EMMANUEL JOSEPH

Career Success: Your Comprehensive Guide to Finding and Securing Your Dream Job

Contents

1

Chapter 1: Introduction to the Job Search Process

D efining Your Career Goals

Embarking on a job search is a significant step in your professional journey. However, before diving into the world of job applications and interviews, it's crucial to take a moment to define your career goals. Knowing what you want to achieve in your career is the first and most critical step in your job search.

Why Career Goals Matter:

- Career goals provide a sense of direction and purpose. They guide your job search efforts by helping you focus on opportunities that align with your aspirations.

- Clarity about your career goals can boost motivation. When you know what you're working towards, you're more likely to stay committed to your job search efforts, even in the face of challenges.

- Defining your goals enables you to make informed decisions. It helps you choose the right job opportunities that will contribute to your long-term career satisfaction.

Assessing Your Interests, Skills, and Values:

Before you can define your career goals, you need to assess your interests, skills, and values. Here's how to do it:

1. Interests: Take some time to reflect on what you're passionate about. What tasks or activities do you enjoy doing? What are your hobbies and interests outside of work? Identifying your interests can help you find a career that aligns with your passions.

2. Skills: Consider your strengths and areas where you excel. What skills do you possess? This could include technical skills, soft skills, or a combination of both. Understanding your strengths is essential in matching them with the right job opportunities.

3. Values: Your values are your guiding principles. What matters most to you in a job? Is it work-life balance, job security, the opportunity for advancement, or making a difference in the world? Identifying your values can help you prioritize job attributes that are in line with what you believe in.

Setting SMART Career Goals:

Once you've assessed your interests, skills, and values, it's time to set SMART (Specific, Measurable, Achievable, Relevant, and Time-bound) career goals. SMART goals are designed to be clear, actionable, and attainable. For example:

- Specific: Define your goal clearly. Instead of saying, "I want a better job," you might say, "I want a managerial role in a tech company that offers opportunities for leadership and professional growth."

- Measurable: Your goal should be quantifiable. Consider how you will measure your progress toward achieving it. For instance, "I aim to increase my annual income by 20% in the next two years."

- Achievable: Your goal should be realistic and attainable. Ensure it's something you have the potential to achieve, given your skills and resources.

- Relevant: Ensure that your goal aligns with your interests, skills, and values. It should be relevant to your overall career aspirations.

- Time-bound: Set a specific timeframe for achieving your goal. "I plan to complete a professional certification within the next six months" is an example of a time-bound goal.

The Benefits of Setting Career Goals:
  - Provides clarity: With well-defined goals, you have a clear direction in your job search, reducing confusion and uncertainty.

- Increases motivation: Goals give you a reason to stay motivated and focused on your job search, even when faced with setbacks.

- Facilitates decision-making: When you have established career goals, you can easily evaluate job opportunities and assess whether they align with your aspirations.

- Aids in long-term planning: Career goals are the foundation of your long-term career plan. They help you create a roadmap for your professional growth.

Remember, your career goals are not set in stone. They can evolve over time as you gain more experience and insights. This chapter has provided you with the foundation for your job search journey. The next chapters will delve into the practical steps you need to take to turn your career goals into reality.

2

Chapter 2: Building a Winning Resume and Cover Letter

Your resume and cover letter are often the first impression you make on potential employers. Crafting these documents effectively is essential in securing job interviews and advancing in your job search. In this chapter, we will explore the elements of a winning resume and cover letter and provide guidance on how to create compelling documents that stand out to employers.

The Role of Your Resume:

Your resume is a snapshot of your professional background. It should provide a concise and well-organized overview of your education, work experience, skills, and accomplishments. A well-crafted resume serves several purposes:

1. Showcasing your qualifications: A resume highlights your qualifications and demonstrates how you meet the requirements of a job.

2. Making a positive first impression: It's often the first document employers review, so it's crucial to make a positive impression.

3. Creating a basis for interviews: Employers use your resume to decide whether to invite you for an interview. A compelling resume can significantly increase your chances.

The Anatomy of an Effective Resume:
  - Contact Information: Your name, phone number, email address, and optionally, your LinkedIn profile or personal website.
  - Objective or Summary: A brief statement summarizing your career goals and what you bring to the table.
  - Education: List your educational qualifications, including the degree earned, institution, and graduation date.
  - Work Experience: Detail your work history, starting with the most recent job and working backward. Include job titles, company names, dates of employment, and key responsibilities and accomplishments.
  - Skills: Highlight relevant skills, including technical skills, soft skills, and certifications.
  - Achievements: Use quantifiable accomplishments to showcase your impact in previous roles. For example, "Increased sales by 20% in the first quarter" or "Managed a team of 10 employees."

The Importance of Tailoring Your Resume:
  Customizing your resume for each job application is vital. Here's how to tailor your resume effectively:

1. Review the job description: Study the job posting and identify key qualifications and skills sought by the employer.

2. Highlight relevant experience: Emphasize experiences and accomplishments that align with the job requirements.

3. Use keywords: Incorporate relevant keywords from the job posting to make your resume more likely to pass through applicant tracking systems (ATS).

Writing an Effective Cover Letter:

A cover letter is your opportunity to introduce yourself, explain your interest in the position, and demonstrate why you're a great fit for the job. Here's how to write an effective cover letter:

1. Address it to a specific person: Whenever possible, address your cover letter to the hiring manager or the person responsible for recruitment.

2. Use a professional format: Start with a formal salutation, such as "Dear Mr. Smith." Follow with a clear and concise introduction explaining your purpose for writing.

3. Highlight your qualifications: Discuss how your skills and experiences make you a strong candidate for the role. Provide specific examples of your achievements.

4. Express enthusiasm: Convey your enthusiasm for the company and the position. Show that you've done your research and are genuinely interested.

5. Close with a call to action: End your cover letter by expressing your desire for an interview and thanking the reader for their time.

6. Proofread and edit: Carefully proofread your cover letter to eliminate errors and ensure clarity.

Resume and Cover Letter Resources:
  - There are numerous online templates and tools that can help you create a visually appealing and well-structured resume.
  - Seek feedback from peers, mentors, or career advisors to improve your documents.
  - Remember that your resume and cover letter are dynamic documents. Update them regularly to reflect your latest accomplishments and skills.

In the next chapter, we will dive into the world of online job boards and how to effectively use them in your job search.

3

Chapter 3: Navigating Online Job Boards

Online job boards have revolutionized the job search process, offering an extensive array of opportunities and resources for job seekers. In this chapter, we will explore how to effectively navigate online job boards to find the job that matches your career goals and interests.

Understanding the Role of Online Job Boards:

Online job boards serve as a central hub for job postings from various industries and organizations. They provide a convenient way to search for job opportunities, research companies, and connect with potential employers. Here's how to make the most of online job boards:

Choosing the Right Job Boards:

Not all job boards are created equal. To maximize your job search efforts, consider the following when selecting the job boards you want to use:

1. Niche vs. General Job Boards: Niche job boards cater to specific industries or professions, offering targeted opportunities. General job boards, like Indeed, LinkedIn, or Monster, cover a wide range of job types.

2. Local vs. National/Global: Decide whether you want to focus on local job opportunities or are open to national or international positions.

3. Industry-Specific Boards: If you're in a specialized field, explore industry-specific job boards that are relevant to your profession.

Setting Up Job Alerts:

Many job boards offer the option to set up job alerts. This is a powerful feature that can save you time and ensure you never miss relevant job postings. Here's how to use job alerts effectively:

1. Define Your Criteria: Specify the job titles, keywords, locations, and other filters relevant to your job search.

2. Frequency: Choose how often you want to receive alerts, such as daily or weekly updates.

3. Review and Adjust: Regularly review the alerts you receive and adjust your criteria as needed. This ensures that you only see the most relevant job postings.

Navigating Search Results:

When you begin your search, it's essential to understand how to navigate search results effectively:

1. Keywords: Use relevant keywords in your search. For example, if you're looking for a marketing job, use terms like "digital marketing manager" or "marketing coordinator."

2. Filters: Most job boards offer filters to refine your search results. These can include location, job type (full-time, part-time, contract), and salary range.

3. Company Research: After identifying interesting job postings, take the

time to research the hiring company. This will help you gauge whether it aligns with your career goals and values.

Optimizing Your Online Profile:

Many job boards allow you to create an online profile or resume that employers can view. Here's how to optimize your online presence:

1. Complete Your Profile: Fill out all relevant sections, including your work history, skills, and certifications.

2. Professional Photo: Use a professional-looking photo that conveys a positive image.

3. Recommendations and Endorsements: Seek recommendations and endorsements from colleagues and mentors to enhance your credibility.

Applying for Jobs:

When you're ready to apply for a job you've found on a job board, be mindful of the following:

1. Customize Your Application: Tailor your resume and cover letter for each application. Address the specific qualifications and requirements mentioned in the job posting.

2. Application Deadlines: Be aware of application deadlines and submit your materials on time.

3. Follow Instructions: Carefully follow the application instructions provided by the employer.

Track Your Progress:

It's a good idea to keep track of the jobs you've applied for, including the date of application, the company name, and the outcome (interview, rejection, etc.). This can help you stay organized during the job search.

Online job boards are valuable tools in your job search toolkit. In the next chapter, we will explore the power of leveraging social media to enhance your job search and expand your professional network.

4

Chapter 4: Leveraging Social Media for Job Hunting

In today's digital age, social media has become a powerful tool for job seekers. It not only offers a platform to connect with potential employers and industry professionals but also provides a means to showcase your skills and personal brand. In this chapter, we'll explore how to effectively leverage social media in your job search.

Creating a Professional Online Presence:

Your social media profiles should project a professional image and reflect your career goals. Here's how to establish a strong online presence:

1. LinkedIn: LinkedIn is the go-to platform for professional networking. Ensure your profile is complete, including a professional photo, detailed work history, skills, and recommendations. Use a compelling headline and summary that clearly state your career objectives.

2. Other Social Media: While LinkedIn is crucial, don't neglect other platforms like Twitter, Instagram, and Facebook. Adjust your privacy settings on personal accounts and focus on showcasing your professional side. Share

relevant content and engage with industry-related posts and discussions.

3. Consistency: Maintain consistency across platforms with consistent profile photos, bios, and a professional tone in your posts.

Networking on Social Media:

Effective networking on social media can open doors to job opportunities. Here's how to connect with professionals and expand your network:

1. Connect Strategically: Send personalized connection requests to professionals in your field. Mention your shared interests or why you'd like to connect.

2. Join Groups and Communities: Participate in LinkedIn groups, Facebook groups, or Twitter chats relevant to your industry. Engage in discussions and share your insights.

3. Engage in Conversations: Comment on and share posts related to your field. Engaging in meaningful conversations can help you build relationships.

4. Direct Messaging: Use direct messages to reach out to contacts for informational interviews or to express your interest in their organization.

Showcasing Your Expertise:

Your social media profiles can serve as a platform to demonstrate your knowledge and expertise. Here's how to showcase your skills:

1. Share Content: Share articles, blog posts, or industry news related to your field. Add your commentary to position yourself as a thought leader.

2. Create Content: Consider starting a blog or vlog to share your insights,

experiences, and tips related to your industry. This can help you stand out as an expert.

3. Participate in Challenges: Many platforms host challenges or contests. Participating in these can help you gain visibility and connect with like-minded professionals.

Finding Job Opportunities:

Social media platforms are increasingly being used to post job openings. Here's how to find job opportunities on social media:

1. Follow Companies: Follow the social media accounts of companies you're interested in working for. Many organizations post job openings on their profiles.

2. Use Hashtags: Search for job-related hashtags on platforms like Twitter and Instagram. This can help you discover job openings and relevant discussions.

3. Engage with Recruiters: Many recruiters actively use social media to identify potential candidates. Engage with them by commenting on their posts and sharing your interest in job opportunities.

Maintaining a Professional Image:

While social media can be a valuable asset in your job search, it's essential to maintain a professional image. Here's how to do that:

1. Clean Up Personal Accounts: Review your personal social media accounts and remove or set privacy settings for content that may not align with your professional image.

2. Think Before You Post: Always think twice before posting. Be mindful of

how your posts and comments may be perceived by potential employers.

3. Avoid Controversial Topics: Steer clear of controversial topics that could potentially harm your job prospects.

Leveraging social media in your job search can be a game-changer. In the next chapter, we'll explore the art of networking and building valuable connections both online and in person.

5

Chapter 5: Networking and Building Connections

Networking is a vital aspect of any successful job search. Whether you're looking for new opportunities, seeking advice, or simply expanding your professional circle, effective networking can open doors to career growth. In this chapter, we will explore the importance of networking and provide guidance on how to build valuable connections both online and in person.

The Power of Networking:

Networking is more than just collecting business cards or connecting on LinkedIn. It's about establishing and nurturing relationships with individuals who can offer support, guidance, and potential opportunities throughout your career. Here's why networking is so essential:

1. Job Opportunities: Many job openings are never publicly advertised. Networking can help you access the hidden job market, where positions are filled through personal connections.

2. Career Advice: Experienced professionals can offer valuable insights,

mentorship, and advice that can accelerate your career growth.

3. Access to Industry Insights: Networking connects you with people who can provide insights into industry trends, market changes, and emerging opportunities.

4. Personal Branding: Building a strong network can enhance your personal brand and reputation within your industry.

Online Networking:

The digital age has expanded networking opportunities to a global scale. Here's how to effectively network online:

1. LinkedIn: Maintain an active and professional presence on LinkedIn. Connect with colleagues, alumni, and industry professionals. Engage in discussions, share relevant content, and use the platform to stay updated on industry news.

2. Twitter: Follow thought leaders and industry experts on Twitter. Participate in relevant Twitter chats and discussions. Use the platform to share your insights and expertise.

3. Facebook and Instagram: While these platforms are less professional, you can still follow companies and organizations of interest. Join relevant groups and engage in discussions where appropriate.

4. Email and Direct Messaging: Reach out to professionals with personalized messages expressing your desire to connect and learn from them.

In-Person Networking:

In-person networking can be just as valuable as online connections. Here's how to make the most of face-to-face interactions:

1. Attend Industry Events: Conferences, seminars, workshops, and trade shows are excellent opportunities to meet professionals in your field. Prepare an elevator pitch to introduce yourself.

2. Join Professional Associations: Membership in industry-specific associations can provide access to networking events, conferences, and workshops.

3. Alumni Events: Many universities and colleges host alumni events. These are great opportunities to connect with people who share your educational background.

4. Local Meetups and Networking Groups: Check for local events and networking groups in your area. These smaller gatherings can facilitate meaningful connections.

Networking Etiquette:

Effective networking requires certain etiquette:

1. Give Before You Receive: Offer support, advice, or assistance to your network without expecting immediate returns. This builds trust and goodwill.

2. Be Genuine: Authenticity is key in networking. Be yourself and establish connections based on shared interests and goals.

3. Follow Up: After meeting someone, follow up with a thank-you email or message. Nurture these relationships over time.

4. Ask for Advice, Not Just Jobs: Don't approach networking contacts solely for job leads. Seek advice, insights, and mentorship, which can naturally lead

to job opportunities.

5. Be Respectful of Time: When asking for a meeting or phone call, respect the other person's time. Be concise and focused during conversations.

Networking is an ongoing process that can be immensely beneficial to your career. As you build and maintain your network, you'll find that opportunities and connections continue to grow. In the next chapter, we'll delve into the importance of researching companies and industries to make informed decisions in your job search.

6

Chapter 6: Researching Companies and Industries

Before you embark on your job search, it's essential to gather insights about the companies and industries you're interested in. Comprehensive research enables you to make informed decisions, present yourself as a well-prepared candidate, and align your career goals with the right organizations. In this chapter, we will explore the importance of researching companies and industries and how to conduct effective research.

The Importance of Company and Industry Research:

1. Alignment with Values: Researching companies helps you identify organizations that align with your values, mission, and workplace culture. This alignment is crucial for job satisfaction and long-term career success.

2. Informed Decision-Making: Informed candidates are better equipped to make the right decisions when choosing job opportunities. Research provides the data and insights you need to assess whether a company is the right fit for you.

3. Preparation for Interviews: Knowing about the company's history,

products or services, industry challenges, and recent achievements allows you to answer interview questions confidently and impress potential employers.

4. Networking: When you network with professionals in your industry, it's essential to have a good understanding of the companies and industries you discuss. It helps you engage in meaningful conversations and build valuable connections.

How to Research Companies:

1. Company Websites: Start with the company's official website. Look for information about their mission, values, history, leadership team, and products or services.

2. Annual Reports: Annual reports can provide valuable financial insights, future strategies, and recent achievements. These reports are usually available on the company's website under the "Investor Relations" section.

3. News and Press Releases: Check for recent news articles and press releases about the company. This will help you understand their recent developments, partnerships, and achievements.

4. Company Culture and Reviews: Explore websites like Glassdoor and Indeed to read employee reviews and get a sense of the company's culture and work environment.

5. LinkedIn: Visit the company's LinkedIn page to see their recent updates, employee profiles, and connections within your network who might work at the company.

6. Social Media: Follow the company on social media platforms to get real-time updates and insights into their activities, values, and culture.

7. Industry Reports: If you're interested in a particular industry, look for industry-specific reports and publications that provide insights into trends, challenges, and key players.

Preparing for Interviews:

Company research is especially valuable when preparing for interviews. Here's how to leverage your research during the interview process:

1. Tailor Your Responses: Use your knowledge about the company to customize your responses to interview questions. Demonstrate how your skills and experience align with the company's goals and values.

2. Ask Informed Questions: Prepare thoughtful questions to ask the interviewer based on your research. This shows your genuine interest in the company and the role.

3. Show Enthusiasm: Incorporate your findings about the company into your conversation to demonstrate your enthusiasm for the opportunity.

Continuous Learning:

Research should be an ongoing process, even after you've secured a job. It's essential to stay updated on industry trends, changes within your company, and new developments in your field. This knowledge will help you adapt and grow throughout your career.

By conducting thorough research on companies and industries, you position yourself as a well-informed and attractive candidate. In the next chapter, we will dive into interview preparation, covering common interview questions and effective strategies for success.

Chapter 7: Preparing for Interviews

Interviews are a critical stage in the job search process. Your performance during an interview can make or break your chances of securing a job. This chapter will guide you through the process of interview preparation, covering various aspects, from understanding different interview formats to effectively answering common interview questions and presenting yourself as the ideal candidate.

Understanding Interview Formats:

Before diving into interview preparation, it's crucial to be aware of different interview formats:

1. One-on-One Interviews: The most common format where you meet with one interviewer. This can be with a hiring manager or a member of the HR team.

2. Panel Interviews: Involves multiple interviewers, typically from different departments within the company. Be prepared to engage with each panel member.

3. Behavioral Interviews: Focus on your past experiences and how they relate

to the job's requirements. Expect questions like "Tell me about a time when you faced a challenging situation at work."

4. Phone and Video Interviews: Increasingly popular due to remote work. Prepare for these by ensuring a quiet, well-lit environment and checking your technology beforehand.

5. Case Interviews: Common in industries like consulting. You'll be presented with a specific problem or case and asked to provide a solution.

Preparing for Common Interview Questions:

Interview questions can cover a wide range of topics. Here are some common questions you should be ready to answer:

1. Tell me about yourself: Prepare a concise and compelling overview of your professional background, focusing on relevant experiences and skills.

2. Why do you want to work here: Discuss what attracts you to the company, such as its culture, values, products, or industry reputation.

3. What are your strengths and weaknesses: Highlight your strengths and discuss how you're actively working on improving any weaknesses.

4. Describe a challenging situation you've faced at work: Use the STAR method (Situation, Task, Action, Result) to structure your response and emphasize problem-solving and personal growth.

5. Where do you see yourself in five years: Talk about your career goals and how they align with the company's growth and opportunities.

6. Why should we hire you: Emphasize your unique qualifications and how they directly benefit the company.

Interview Preparation Strategies:

1. Research the Company: Study the company's history, mission, values, products, and recent developments. Understanding their culture and objectives will allow you to tailor your responses.

2. Understand the Job Description: Analyze the job posting, identifying the key qualifications and responsibilities. Be prepared to connect your skills and experience to these requirements.

3. Practice Your Responses: Prepare answers to common questions and practice your responses. You can do this with a trusted friend, family member, or a career coach.

4. Create Questions for the Interviewer: Craft thoughtful questions to ask the interviewer about the company, team, or role. This shows your genuine interest.

5. Dress for Success: Select appropriate attire based on the company culture and industry norms. When in doubt, it's better to be slightly overdressed.

6. Gather Necessary Documents: Bring extra copies of your resume, a list of references, and any requested documents or certifications.

7. Plan Your Route: If it's an in-person interview, plan your route and arrive early. If it's a virtual interview, ensure your technology is functioning correctly.

During the Interview:

1. Stay Calm and Confident: Maintain a calm and confident demeanor throughout the interview. Remember that interviews are also an opportunity for you to assess whether the company is a good fit for you.

2. Active Listening: Pay close attention to the interviewer's questions and comments. This will help you respond effectively and demonstrate your listening skills.

3. Non-Verbal Communication: Be mindful of your body language. Maintain eye contact, offer a firm handshake, and sit up straight (in the case of in-person interviews).

Follow-Up:

After the interview, send a thank-you email to express your appreciation for the opportunity and reiterate your interest in the position. This is a chance to reaffirm your enthusiasm and leave a positive impression.

Effective interview preparation increases your confidence and enhances your chances of success. In the next chapter, we will delve into the world of online job applications and how to present yourself effectively through these platforms.

8

Chapter 8: Mastering the Online Application Process

Online job applications have become the norm in the job search process. Mastering this process is essential to successfully apply for jobs, stand out as a candidate, and increase your chances of getting employed. In this chapter, we'll explore strategies for effectively navigating the online application process.

Understanding the Online Application Process:

Online job applications vary from one employer to another, but there are common elements you'll encounter during this process:

1. Create User Accounts: Many companies require you to create a user account or profile on their website or applicant tracking system (ATS).

2. Resume and Cover Letter Upload: You'll typically be asked to upload your resume and cover letter. Ensure that these documents are tailored to the specific job you're applying for.

3. Application Forms: Complete online forms with your personal and

professional information. Be thorough and accurate in your responses.

4. Questionnaires and Assessments: Some applications include questionnaires or assessments to evaluate your skills or personality traits.

5. References: Provide references if requested. Make sure you've obtained permission from your references in advance.

Strategies for Effective Online Applications:

1. Prepare Your Documents: Have your resume and cover letter ready in formats that are widely accepted (e.g., PDF or Word). Tailor them for each application to match the job description.

2. Create a Master Resume: Maintain a detailed master resume that includes all your work experience, skills, and achievements. When applying for a job, select and edit relevant sections from this master document.

3. Review the Job Posting: Carefully read the job posting and requirements. Customize your application materials to address the specific qualifications and responsibilities mentioned in the posting.

4. Use Keywords: Incorporate relevant keywords from the job description in your resume and application. Many companies use applicant tracking systems (ATS) that scan for keywords to filter candidates.

5. Complete All Fields: Fill out all fields in the application form, even those marked as optional. Incomplete applications may be disregarded.

6. Double-Check for Errors: Proofread your application thoroughly to eliminate typos and grammatical errors. A well-crafted, error-free application is more likely to stand out.

7. Maintain Consistency: Ensure consistency between your resume, cover letter, and the information provided in the application form. Inconsistencies can raise red flags.

8. Save a Copy: Save a copy of the completed application or take screenshots for your records. This can be helpful if you're invited for an interview or if you need to follow up.

9. Be Prompt: Apply as soon as possible after the job posting goes live. Some positions have application deadlines, and early applicants may have an advantage.

Applicant Tracking Systems (ATS):

Many companies use ATS to manage and filter job applications. Understanding how ATS works can give you an edge:

1. Keyword Optimization: ATS often scan for specific keywords, so include relevant terms from the job description in your application.

2. Clean Formatting: Use simple, clean formatting in your resume to ensure the ATS can read it accurately.

3. Avoid Graphics and Tables: Complicated graphics, tables, or unusual formatting can confuse ATS. Stick to standard formats.

4. PDF Format: Save your documents in PDF format. This maintains formatting and is easily readable by ATS.

Follow-Up:

After submitting an online application, it's a good practice to follow up with the employer. You can send a polite email expressing your interest in the position and inquiring about the status of your application.

Effectively mastering the online application process is a crucial step in your job search. In the next chapter, we will explore the benefits of job fairs and career events and how to make the most of them in your quest for employment.

9

Chapter 9: Maximizing Job Fairs and Career Events

Job fairs and career events are valuable opportunities to connect with potential employers, learn about different companies and industries, and make a lasting impression on recruiters. In this chapter, we will explore the benefits of attending job fairs and career events and provide strategies to make the most of these occasions.

The Benefits of Job Fairs and Career Events:

1. Face-to-Face Interaction: Job fairs provide the chance to meet recruiters and hiring managers in person, which can help you create a memorable impression that's often difficult to achieve through online applications.

2. Explore Multiple Opportunities: At a single job fair, you can explore opportunities with multiple employers across various industries, making it an efficient way to job search.

3. Company Insights: You can gain valuable insights about companies, their cultures, and their hiring processes by engaging in conversations with representatives.

4. Networking: Job fairs are excellent places to network with professionals in your industry, including potential mentors or colleagues.

5. Learn About Trends: You can stay updated on industry trends, requirements, and emerging job opportunities.

Strategies for Maximizing Job Fairs and Career Events:

1. Research Participating Companies: Prior to the event, research the list of participating companies. Identify those that align with your career goals and interests.

2. Prepare Your Elevator Pitch: Craft a concise and engaging elevator pitch that introduces yourself, your background, and your career aspirations. Practice this pitch before the event.

3. Dress Professionally: Dress in professional attire appropriate for the industry and company culture. First impressions matter.

4. Bring Multiple Resumes: Prepare a stack of well-crafted resumes tailored to the companies you're targeting. Have more resumes on hand than you expect to distribute.

5. Prepare Questions: Develop a list of thoughtful questions to ask recruiters. This shows your genuine interest and knowledge about the company.

6. Prioritize Your Time: While it's essential to explore different opportunities, prioritize your time and focus on your top-choice companies.

7. Follow Event Guidelines: Adhere to any guidelines or instructions provided by the event organizers. This may include registering online, arriving at a specific time, or following a particular process.

8. Engage Actively: Approach each booth with a confident and friendly demeanor. Shake hands, introduce yourself, and express your interest in their organization.

9. Collect Business Cards: Obtain business cards from recruiters or representatives you speak with. These can be used for follow-up communications.

10. Take Notes: After each interaction, jot down key points or unique insights about the company or role. This will help you remember important details when you follow up.

11. Follow Up: After the event, send personalized thank-you emails to the recruiters you spoke with. Mention your conversation and your interest in the company.

Additional Tips for Success:

- Be open to exploring new opportunities and industries. You may discover a passion for something you hadn't considered before.

- Attend workshops or seminars that are often part of job fairs and career events. They can provide valuable information and networking opportunities.

- Be patient and maintain a positive attitude, even if you face rejection or don't find the perfect fit immediately.

Job fairs and career events are dynamic environments that can significantly enhance your job search. They offer a unique chance to make a personal connection with employers and other professionals. In the next chapter, we will explore the role of recruiters and staffing agencies in the job search process.

10

Chapter 10: Working with Recruiters and Staffing Agencies

Recruiters and staffing agencies play a crucial role in connecting job seekers with employers. They often have access to job opportunities that may not be publicly advertised. In this chapter, we will explore the benefits of working with recruiters and staffing agencies, as well as strategies to effectively engage with them in your job search.

The Role of Recruiters and Staffing Agencies:

1. Access to Hidden Job Market: Recruiters have access to job openings that are not publicly advertised, giving you an advantage in finding opportunities.

2. Expertise in Industry and Market: They often specialize in specific industries, allowing them to provide insights into market trends and job requirements.

3. Matchmaking: Recruiters aim to find the right fit for both job seekers and employers. They can help you find positions that align with your skills and career goals.

4. Streamlined Process: Working with a recruiter can streamline the job application process, as they assist in preparing your application and scheduling interviews.

Strategies for Effective Engagement:

1. Identify Specialized Recruiters: Look for recruiters or staffing agencies that specialize in your industry or profession. They are more likely to have relevant job opportunities.

2. Build a Relationship: Establish a professional relationship with recruiters. Attend networking events or job fairs where you can meet them in person.

3. Update Your Resume: Ensure your resume is up-to-date and tailored to the type of positions you are seeking. Provide recruiters with the most accurate and compelling representation of your skills and experience.

4. Be Clear About Your Goals: Communicate your career goals and expectations clearly with your recruiter. This includes the type of roles you're interested in, salary expectations, and preferred company culture.

5. Follow Up: Regularly follow up with your recruiter to stay informed about job opportunities. Be proactive in expressing your continued interest.

6. Prepare for Interviews: Just as you would for any job application, prepare thoroughly for interviews arranged by recruiters. Research the company and practice your interview skills.

7. Provide References: Have a list of professional references ready to share with your recruiter. Ensure that these individuals are aware that they may be contacted.

8. Negotiate Offers: If a job offer is extended through the recruiter, work

with them to negotiate the terms and conditions.

Maintain Realistic Expectations:

It's important to keep in mind that working with recruiters and staffing agencies does not guarantee immediate job placement. Be patient, as the process can take time, and your recruiter may present multiple opportunities before you find the right fit.

Choosing the Right Recruiter:

Not all recruiters are the same. Consider the following factors when selecting a recruiter or staffing agency:

1. Reputation: Research their reputation in the industry and read reviews or testimonials if available.

2. Experience: Find out how long they've been in the industry and if they have a track record of successful placements.

3. Communication: Assess their communication style and responsiveness. You want a recruiter who keeps you informed.

4. Specialization: Ensure they specialize in your field or industry for the best match.

5. Ethical Practices: Verify that they follow ethical and transparent business practices.

Recruiters and staffing agencies can be valuable allies in your job search. When working with them, maintain professionalism and open communication to increase your chances of finding the right job opportunity. In the next chapter, we will explore the importance of continuous learning and skill development to advance your career.

11

Chapter 11: Continuous Learning and Skill Development

In today's fast-paced job market, the importance of continuous learning and skill development cannot be overstated. Employers value candidates who are adaptable and committed to improving their skills. In this chapter, we will explore the significance of ongoing education and skill enhancement and how they can help you advance in your career.

The Importance of Continuous Learning:

1. Stay Relevant: Industries and job requirements evolve rapidly. Continuous learning ensures that you remain up-to-date and relevant in your field.

2. Professional Growth: Acquiring new skills and knowledge can open doors to higher-paying positions and career advancement.

3. Adapt to Change: In a dynamic job market, adaptability is a valuable trait. Learning new skills and technologies helps you embrace change more effectively.

4. Increased Job Security: Employees who invest in their own development

are often seen as more valuable and are less likely to be laid off during economic downturns.

Strategies for Continuous Learning and Skill Development:

1. Online Courses: There are numerous online platforms, such as Coursera, edX, and LinkedIn Learning, offering a wide range of courses in various fields. Consider enrolling in courses that align with your career goals.

2. Certifications: Earning industry-recognized certifications can enhance your resume and demonstrate your expertise to employers. Research certifications that are relevant to your profession.

3. Conferences and Workshops: Attend industry-specific conferences, workshops, and seminars. These events provide opportunities for networking and hands-on learning.

4. Professional Associations: Join professional associations related to your field. Many of them offer resources, webinars, and events for members.

5. Mentorship: Seek out mentors who can provide guidance, share insights, and help you develop your skills. Mentorship relationships can be invaluable for career growth.

6. Reading and Research: Stay informed about industry trends and developments by reading books, research papers, blogs, and industry-specific publications.

7. Online Forums and Discussion Groups: Participate in online forums and discussion groups related to your profession. Engage in conversations and share your knowledge.

8. Soft Skills: Don't forget the importance of developing soft skills like

communication, leadership, and problem-solving. These skills are highly sought after by employers.

Setting Learning Goals:

1. Identify Your Goals: Clearly define what you want to achieve through continuous learning. Whether it's to qualify for a promotion or transition into a new field, knowing your goals will help you select the right learning opportunities.

2. Create a Plan: Develop a learning plan with specific steps, timelines, and resources. Break your goals into smaller, manageable milestones.

3. Accountability: Share your learning goals with a mentor, friend, or family member who can hold you accountable.

4. Measure Progress: Regularly assess your progress toward your learning goals. Adjust your plan as needed based on your achievements and any new developments in your field.

Balancing Learning with Work:

Balancing a full-time job with continuous learning can be challenging, but it's essential for your career growth. Consider these strategies:

1. Time Management: Allocate specific times for learning and stick to your schedule.

2. Online Learning: Take advantage of online courses that offer flexibility, allowing you to learn at your own pace.

3. Lunch Breaks: Use lunch breaks or downtime at work for short learning activities, like reading articles or watching brief tutorials.

4. Prioritize Tasks: Prioritize your most important learning goals and focus on them during your available time.

5. Invest in Your Future: Consider your learning and skill development as an investment in your future.

Stay Curious:

Curiosity is a powerful driver for continuous learning. Cultivate a curious mindset, and embrace new challenges and opportunities to expand your knowledge and skills.

By continuously learning and improving your skill set, you'll not only become a more attractive candidate to potential employers but also enhance your overall job satisfaction and career prospects. In the next chapter, we will explore the art of crafting a compelling resume and cover letter that effectively represent your qualifications and aspirations.

12

Chapter 12: Crafting an Effective Resume and Cover Letter

Your resume and cover letter are your first opportunity to make a strong impression on potential employers. A well-crafted resume and cover letter can significantly increase your chances of getting noticed and landing an interview. In this chapter, we will explore the art of creating a compelling resume and cover letter that effectively represent your qualifications and aspirations.

Creating an Impactful Resume:

1. Clear Formatting: Keep your resume format clean and organized. Use clear headings, bullet points, and a consistent font style.

2. Tailor for Each Job: Customize your resume for each job application by highlighting relevant skills and experiences. Use keywords from the job posting.

3. Contact Information: Include your full name, professional email address, and phone number. You can omit personal details like age and marital status.

4. Professional Summary: Write a concise professional summary at the beginning, summarizing your skills, experience, and career objectives.

5. Work Experience: List your work experience in reverse chronological order, starting with your most recent job. Include the company name, location, your job title, and specific accomplishments or responsibilities for each role.

6. Education: Include your educational background, starting with your most recent degree. Mention the institution, degree earned, graduation date, and any relevant honors or achievements.

7. Skills: Create a section for your key skills, including technical skills, certifications, and languages.

8. Achievements: Highlight your achievements, such as awards, publications, or significant projects. Quantify your achievements whenever possible.

9. Relevance: Ensure that the content of your resume directly relates to the job you're applying for. Irrelevant information can clutter your resume.

Writing an Effective Cover Letter:

1. Address the Hiring Manager: Whenever possible, address your cover letter to the hiring manager by name. Avoid generic salutations like "To Whom It May Concern."

2. Customization: Customize your cover letter for each job application. Mention the specific job title and company name in the opening paragraph.

3. Opening Paragraph: Begin with a strong opening that introduces yourself and explains why you're interested in the position.

4. Show Your Value: Describe how your skills and experiences align with the job requirements and how you can bring value to the company.

5. Accomplishments: Mention key accomplishments from your past roles that are relevant to the job you're applying for. Be specific and use quantifiable data when possible.

6. Passion for the Company: Express your enthusiasm for the company and explain why you're excited about the opportunity.

7. Closing Paragraph: Summarize your interest in the position and express your desire for an interview. Thank the employer for considering your application.

8. Professional Tone: Maintain a professional and positive tone throughout the cover letter. Avoid negative or critical language.

9. Proofreading: Carefully proofread your cover letter to eliminate errors in spelling, grammar, and punctuation. Mistakes can leave a negative impression.

Additional Tips:

- Keep both your resume and cover letter concise, ideally within one page each.
  - Use action verbs to describe your accomplishments in your resume.
  - Avoid using jargon or overly technical language that the employer may not understand.
  - Utilize white space and bullet points to make your documents more readable.
  - Incorporate your personal branding or unique selling points in both your resume and cover letter.

Customize, Customize, Customize:

The key to an effective resume and cover letter is customization. Tailor both documents for each job application to highlight your qualifications, demonstrate your enthusiasm for the position, and make a memorable impression.

Crafting compelling resumes and cover letters is an ongoing process, and you should continuously update them as your career progresses. These documents are vital tools in your job search toolkit and should be used strategically to help you stand out among other applicants.